Longman English Guides

GRAMMAR

S H Burton

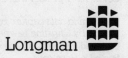

Longman

Titles in the series

ABC of Common Errors   *S H Burton*

Writing Letters   *S H Burton*

Punctuation   *Ian Gordon*

Spelling   *S H Burton*

Help Yourself to Study   *Lesley Millard & Ralph Tabberer*

LONGMAN GROUP UK LIMITED,
Longman House,
Burnt Mill, Harlow, Essex CM20 2JE, England
and Associated Companies throughout the world.

First published 1987

ISBN 0 582 25096 X

Set in 10/11 pt Rockwell light and medium

Editing and data capture by Stenton Associates
Design by Christine Lawrie
Produced by Longman Group (FE) Ltd
Printed in Hong Kong

CONTENTS

INTRODUCTION

You do not need to have any previous knowledge of grammar to make full use of this book for beginners. It sets out the bedrock facts – all of them, and nothing else.

It explains the structure of the English sentence and the parts that individual words and phrases play in that structure. Any advanced grammar studies you may need to make later will be an extension of what you learn from this book.

I want to say just two more things about it. First, it is a book you can use on your own. The explanations are made in straightforward language and illustrated with plenty of examples. Second, practice exercises are provided so that you can check your understanding of each point. Answers are given at the end of the book, but try to find your own answers before you look at mine.

S H Burton

1
THE SENTENCE

1

> A SENTENCE is a group of words put together so that it makes complete sense.

Examples

1. The bus is stopping.
2. She hid her savings book.
3. That firm sells records.
4. The last mile tired the runners.
5. I posted her present.
6. We went home.

2 A sentence may include a PHRASE or PHRASES.

Examples

1. The bus is stopping *at the lights*.
2. She hid her savings book *under a pile of old newspapers*.
3. That firm sells records *at bargain prices*.
4. The last mile *over rough ground* tired the runners.
5. I posted her present *just before Christmas*.
6. *After the party* we went home *by taxi*.

3 The difference between a sentence and a phrase is that a sentence makes complete sense ON ITS OWN, but a phrase does not.

4   A phrase is part of a sentence. It adds to (enlarges) the meaning of the sentence in which it is included. (See Section 19.)

REMEMBER
- A SENTENCE is an independent, self-contained unit.
- It makes complete sense without needing the help of any other words.
- A group of words that does not make complete sense until other words have been added to it is NOT a sentence.

- A PHRASE is not an independent, self-contained unit.
- Its function is to enlarge the meaning of the sentence of which it forms a part.

Practice 1

Which of the following examples are sentences?

1 John Brown left his keys.
2 In his car.
3 Then he slammed the driver's door.
4 With the catch down.
5 He was locked out.
6 The local garage could not supply a duplicate key.
7 For that particular model.
8 He made enquiries.
9 At the police station.
10 After a long time.
11 They opened the car door.
12 With a lot of trouble.

Practice 2

Combine the examples in Practice 1 to form a continuous passage of six sentences. Include each of the phrases in the sentence where it makes most sense.

6

2
SUBJECT AND PREDICATE

1 | Every sentence consists of two parts: its SUBJECT and its PREDICATE.

2 The SUBJECT names or identifies the person, place, thing or idea that the sentence is about.

Examples

All the words that form the SUBJECT of each sentence are in CAPITALS.

1 BIRDS fly.
2 MARY answered the phone.
3 A NEW HOUSING ESTATE is being planned.
4 BUYING A SECONDHAND CAR can be risky.
5 Very slowly, HE recovered his health.

REMEMBER The name 'subject' explains what the SUBJECT of a sentence does. The SUBJECT of a sentence tells us what the subject (the topic) of the sentence is.

3 **THE PREDICATE** contains all the words that say something about the person, place, thing or idea named in the subject of a sentence.

Examples

All the words that form the PREDICATE of each sentence are in *italics*. The words in the SUBJECT are in CAPITALS.

1 WATER *freezes*.
2 *That night* THE PIPES *burst*.
3 *After several attempts*, WE *got it going*.
4 THE RESULTS OF THE TEST *will be known next week*.
5 THE RUNNING COSTS OF THE NEW MACHINE *have been underestimated*.

REMEMBER The PREDICATE states something about the SUBJECT.

Example

The old man's coat was threadbare.

The words *The old man's coat* tell us what the sentence is about. They form the SUBJECT of the sentence.

The words *was threadbare* state something about the subject. They form the PREDICATE of the sentence.

4 A group of words cannot make complete sense unless it contains both a subject and a predicate.

Example

All the schools closed yesterday.

subject	+	*predicate*
All the schools	+	closed yesterday

The subject cannot make complete sense without the predicate.

The predicate cannot make complete sense without the subject.

REMEMBER Although the subject often comes first in a sentence, it need not. Part of the predicate may come before the subject. Several examples have been given

already. Here is another: *On wet days* THE BEACHES
were deserted.

Practice 3

Split each of these sentences into its subject and its
predicate.

Example

This year's apple crop will be very poor.

subject	predicate
This year's apple crop	will be very poor

1. Diesel engines are usually reliable.
2. As yet, the judges have not announced their decision.
3. We are open until eight tonight.
4. His cooking has improved.
5. The two parts of every sentence are the subject and
   the predicate.

4/5

4   HIS COOKING

3
THE PARTS OF SPEECH

1 | Each word in a sentence does a particular job. According to the kind of job it does, it is a particular PART OF SPEECH.

2 There are eight parts of speech.

1 noun   2 pronoun   3 adjective   4 verb
5 adverb   6 conjunction   7 preposition
8 interjection

REMEMBER
- The WORK that a word does IN A SENTENCE makes it a particular part of speech.
- The same word may act as one part of speech in one sentence and as a different part of speech in another sentence.

Examples

1 The *fish* are disappearing from this bay.

The word *fish* is used as a 'naming' word. It is a NOUN in that sentence.

2 Too many boats *fish* here.

The word *fish* states what the subject of the sentence does. It is a VERB in that sentence.

4
NOUNS

1 | **A NOUN is a naming word.**

2 **Nouns name**
   persons
   places
   things
   ideas, qualities, feelings or states of mind – things
   that exist only in the mind and cannot be seen,
   heard, touched, tasted or smelt – for example:
   'enthusiasm', 'honesty', 'anger'.

Examples

Each noun is in *italics*.

1 *William* flew to *Paris*.
2 The *plane* took off late because the *weather* was bad.
3 The *crew* told the *passengers* that *safety* mattered
  more than *punctuality*.

Practice 4

Find the nouns in these two passages. There are five
nouns in (1) and three nouns in (2).

1 Jack had a fever and a cough, but the doctor said that
  his illness was not serious.
2 Archimedes solved many theoretical and practical
  problems and is still known for his wisdom.

5
PRONOUNS

1

> A PRONOUN stands in for a NOUN. It acts for or in place of a noun.

Examples

Each pronoun is in *italics*.

1 Liz told the waiter that *she* was hungry.

she stands for the noun *Liz*: *she* is a PRONOUN.

2 The waiter assured Liz that *he* would bring the soup to *her* as soon as *it* was ready.

he stands for the noun *waiter*: *he* is a PRONOUN.
her stands for the noun *Liz*: *her* is a PRONOUN.
it stands for the noun *soup*: *it* is a PRONOUN.

2 A pronoun may stand in for a noun used earlier in the sentence, as in the examples above. It may stand in for a noun used later in the sentence.

Examples

Each pronoun is in *italics*.

1 Having tried hard to undo *it*, Jane finally cut the string.

The pronoun *it* stands for the noun *string*.

2 Soak *them* in cold water for at least an hour before cooking the beans for twenty minutes.

The pronoun *them* stands for the noun *beans*.

3   A pronoun may stand in for a noun used in another sentence.

Examples

Each pronoun is in *italics*.

Johnson never got up early. Most nights *he* stayed up late, talking. Morning visitors did not expect *him* to be up and dressed. *They* usually found *him* having breakfast in bed.

4   A pronoun may point to someone or something. When a pronoun stands in for a noun, it means the person or thing that the noun would have named if it had been used.

Examples

Each pronoun is in *italics*.

1 *Those* at the back of the stall are fresher than *these* at the front.
2 Mrs Smith liked both calculators but she chose *this*, though *that* was cheaper.

5   A pronoun may be used in asking a question.

Examples

Each pronoun is in *italics*.

1 *Which* do you prefer?
2 *Who* told you that absurd story?
3 *What* can I say?
4 *Whose* is that car?

6
ADJECTIVES

1

> AN ADJECTIVE is a word used to describe the
> person, place, thing or idea named by a noun.

2   As a convenient 'shorthand' expression it is generally
said that 'an adjective describes a noun'.
In strict grammatical terms, an adjective is said to
QUALIFY ('add qualities to') a noun.

Examples

Each adjective is in *italics*.

1 The *red* notebook is on the *top* shelf.

   The adjective *red* qualifies (describes) the noun
   notebook.
   The adjective *top* qualifies (describes) the noun *shelf*.

2 The *young* Napoleon received the cheers of the
victorious army with *great* delight.

   The adjective *young* qualifies (describes) the noun
   Napoleon.
   The adjective *victorious* qualifies (describes) the
   noun *army*.
   The adjective *great* qualifies (describes) the noun
   delight.

REMEMBER   It is the WORK that a word does IN A SEN-
   TENCE that matters. A word may be an adjective in one
   sentence and a different part of speech in another
   sentence.

Examples

1 Try to write plain English.

   plain is an adjective.

2 A city was built on the fertile plain.

   plain is a noun.

3 Is this the York train?

   York is an adjective.

4 When is the next train to York?

   York is a noun.

3 An adjective often comes immediately before the noun that it qualifies (describes), as in all the examples given so far, but it may be placed somewhere else in the sentence.

Examples

1 The idea seems silly to me.

   The adjective *silly* qualifies (describes) the noun *idea*.

2 The candidate, inexperienced and nervous, was heckled.

   The adjective *inexperienced* qualifies (describes) the noun *candidate*.
   The adjective *nervous* qualifies (describes) the noun *candidate*.

4 Sometimes an adjective points to or points out the noun that it qualifies (describes).

15

Examples

1 *These* shoes will fit me.
2 Sit in *that* chair.

5 **Sometimes an adjective shows the ownership of the noun it qualifies (describes).**

Examples

1 *My* car is being serviced today.
2 The travellers put *their* cases on the rack.
3 Jean is like *her* mother.

6 **Sometimes an adjective helps the noun it qualifies to ask a question.**

Examples

1 *Which* way are you going?
2 *What* instrument does he play?

REMEMBER An adjective does NOT take the place of a noun. That is the work of a pronoun. An adjective always QUALIFIES (describes) a noun.

Examples

1 *Which* book did you choose?

   Which is an adjective in that sentence.

2 *Which* did you choose?

   Which is a pronoun in that sentence.

3 *That* house is *ours*.

   That is an adjective in that sentence; *ours* is a pronoun

7   Although *the* and *a* (or *an*) do the work of adjectives by qualifying (describing) nouns, they are given special names.

They are called the ARTICLES.

The is called the DEFINITE ARTICLE.

A (or *an*) is called the INDEFINITE ARTICLE.

Practice 5

List the adjectives in these sentences. (Do not include the articles.) Identify the noun that each adjective qualifies (describes).

1 His record lasted ten years.
2 The fresh flowers soon faded in that hot room.
3 Did many people come to your birthday party?
4 What car have you got?
5 Their house looks lovely now.

Practice 6

List all the pronouns and all the adjectives in these sentences. There are nine pronouns and eight adjectives.

1 Is that coat yours?
2 Their sketches are excellent and I cannot decide whether to buy his or hers.
3 The tipsters are picking that horse, but I think this will win.
4 Jones did not have much money to begin with and soon he had very little.
5 Anybody can have this rotten job.

Practice 7

List all the nouns in this passage. There are nine.

Gradually, Jo got to know London well. She studied her maps and explored the streets, squares and parks of the capital. Growing familiarity gave her confidence.

7
VERBS

1
> A VERB is the most important word in the PREDI-
> CATE of a sentence.

2   A verb is the most important word in the predicate
because it makes the most important statement about
the subject of the sentence. Without a verb, the predicate cannot do its work. It cannot say something about
the subject. (See Section 2 for an explanation of subject
and predicate.)

3   A verb is either a 'doing' verb or a 'being' verb.

Examples

The SUBJECT of each sentence is in CAPITALS.
The VERB in each sentence is in *italics*.

'doing' verbs
1 THE CAR THIEF *used* a piece of bent wire.
2 HE *drove* through the town.
3 At the motorway slip road TWO POLICEMEN *stopped*
the stolen car.

'being' verbs
1 THE RESULTS OF THE OPINION POLLS *are*
depressing.
2 OUR POLICIES *seem* unpopular.
3 SOME OF OUR LEADING POLITICIANS *became*
deeply disliked last year.

In those three examples, the verbs *are, seem* and *became* tell us about the subjects' state of being. They are 'being' verbs, not 'doing' verbs.

REMEMBER
- Every sentence must contain a subject and a predicate.
- Every predicate must contain a verb.
- Therefore every sentence must contain a verb.

4   A verb often consists of more than one word.

Examples

1 You *will find* your way easily with this map.
2 All my sweets *were eaten* by that greedy brat.
3 She *is running* the race of her life.
4 Hundreds of books *have been written* about Shakespeare, and dozens more *will have been written* about him by the year 2000.

5   The verb tells us WHEN the subject's 'doing' or 'being' takes place. This is called the TENSE of the verb.
     The verb may state that 'doing' or 'being' takes place in the PRESENT (PRESENT TENSE).
     The verb may state that 'doing' or 'being' took place in the PAST (PAST TENSE).
     The verb may state that 'doing' or 'being' will take place in the FUTURE (FUTURE TENSE).

Examples

1 He *runs* every day. (present tense)
2 He *ran* in the race last year. (past tense)
3 He *will run* next year. (future tense)

REMEMBER   TENSE means 'time'.

19

6   The verb also tells us whether the subject does something or whether something is done to the subject.
Or, to put it another way, the verb tells us
whether the subject ACTS – an ACTIVE verb
or
whether the subject IS ACTED UPON – a PASSIVE verb.

Examples

1 The porter *unlocks* the door at six.

> subject: *the porter*
> verb: *unlocks*
> The verb is ACTIVE. It tells us that the subject does something – acts.

2 The door *is unlocked* by the porter at six.

> subject: *the door*
> verb: *is unlocked*
> The verb is PASSIVE. It tells us that the subject has something done to it – is acted upon.

REMEMBER

- When the verb tells us that its subject does something – acts – it is an ACTIVE verb.
- When the verb tells us that the subject has something done to it – is acted upon – it is a PASSIVE verb.

Examples

1 We stopped at the barrier.

> subject: *we*
> verb (active): *stopped*

2 We were stopped at the barrier.

> subject: *we*
> verb (passive): *were stopped*

7   Like all the other parts of speech, a verb can be
     recognised only by the WORK that it does IN A
     SENTENCE.
     A word may be a verb in one sentence and a different
     part of speech in another sentence.

Examples

     1 He turned out of the *drive* much too fast.

        drive names something: it is a NOUN in that sentence.

     2 They *drive* ten miles to work.

        drive tells us what the subject does: it is a VERB in
        that sentence.

Practice 8

     Find the verbs in these sentences. Identify the subject
     of each verb.

     1 For more than a hundred years ships have been built
       in this yard.
     2 She looks fine after her operation.
     3 All the food has been eaten.
     4 Next week the store will be closed for the annual
       holiday.
     5 You will need warm clothes.

8
ADVERBS

1

> An ADVERB is a word used to describe a verb.

2   That is a convenient 'shorthand' way of saying that an
     adverb is a word used to give additional information
     about the action of a verb.
     In strict grammatical terms, an adverb is said to MODIFY
     a verb.

Examples

   1 The door opened *slowly*.

     slowly tells us HOW the action of the verb *opened*
     was performed: *slowly* is an ADVERB.

   2 The plane arrived *late*.

     late tells us WHEN the action of the verb *arrived* was
     performed: *late* is an ADVERB.

   3 I shall plant a tree *there*.

     there tells us WHERE the action of the verb *shall
     plant* will be performed: *there* is an ADVERB.

   4 *Twice*, the whistle was blown.

     Twice tells us HOW MANY TIMES the action of the
     verb *was blown* was performed: *twice* is an ADVERB.

   5 The garden suffered *much* in the bitter weather.

     much tells us TO WHAT EXTENT the action of the
     verb *suffered* was performed: *much* is an ADVERB.

REMEMBER

- An adverb may – and often does – end with *ly* (see *slowly* in sentence 1 above). But an adverb need not end with *ly* (see *late, there, twice* and *much* in the other examples).
- You cannot tell by the look of a word that it is an adverb. You can recognise it as an adverb only by the WORK it does IN A SENTENCE.

3   Like all the other parts of speech, an adverb is recognised by the work that it does. A word may be an adverb in one sentence and a different part of speech in another sentence.

Examples

1 The work went *well*.

   well modifies (describes) the verb *went*: it is an ADVERB.

2 The *well* was drained by evening.

   well names something: it is a NOUN.

3 The *well* water was not fit to drink.

   well qualifies (describes) the noun *water*: it is an ADJECTIVE.

4   An adverb may be used to help a verb to ask a question.

Examples

1 *How* shall we recognise him?
2 *Where* do they live?
3 *When* will you know the answer?

23

REMEMBER An adverb modifies (describes) a verb by telling us more about the action of the verb.

Practice 9

Find the adverbs in these sentences. There are eight. State which verb each adverb modifies (describes).

1 He was coughing badly yesterday.
2 Now I know the answer.
3 If you ring once he will hear.
4 A low pressure system remained stationary overhead.
5 Finally we abandoned the search.
6 Where is the salt?

5 **An adverb may also be used to modify (describe) another adverb or an adjective.**

Examples

1 The time passed *very* quickly.

   quickly modifies (describes) the verb *passed*: *quickly* is an ADVERB.
   very modifies (describes) the adverb *quickly*: *very* is an ADVERB.

2 We are *nearly* there.

   there modifies (describes) the verb *are*: *there* is an ADVERB.
   nearly modifies (describes) the adverb *there*: *nearly* is an ADVERB.

3 *Almost* immediately stocks of the new model disappeared from the dealers' showrooms.

   immediately modifies (describes) the verb *disappeared*: *immediately* is an ADVERB.
   Almost modifies (describes) the adverb *immediately*: *Almost* is an ADVERB.

4 That seems an *extremely* interesting idea.

interesting qualifies (describes) the noun *idea*: *interesting* is an ADJECTIVE.
extremely modifies (describes) the adjective *interesting*: *extremely* is an ADVERB.

5 His work is *barely* adequate.

adequate qualifies (describes) the noun *work*: *adequate* is an ADJECTIVE.
barely modifies (describes) the adjective *adequate*: *barely* is an ADVERB.

6 **The word *not* always does the work of an adverb. It modifies (describes) a verb, an adverb, or an adjective. It describes them by making them NEGATIVE. That is why it is called the ADVERB OF NEGATION.**

Examples

1 I shall *not* go to the match tomorrow.
2 His supporters turned out, but *not* enthusiastically.
3 Their defeat in the last round was *not* surprising.

25

9
CONJUNCTIONS

1 | A CONJUNCTION is a word used to join two words or two groups of words together.

2 A conjunction may be used to join one word to another.

Example

Fish *and* chips are sold here.

3 A conjunction may be used to join one phrase to another.

Example

Payment should be made by cheque *or* by postal order.

4 A conjunction may be used to join two sentences together to make one sentence.

Example

He tried hard. He was beaten.
He tried hard *but* he was beaten.

Practice 10

List the five conjunctions used in these sentences.

1 Fred, Jill and Tom used to work here but Tom left a year ago.
2 Will you have this or that?
3 Neither at Christmas nor in the summer could we afford to take time off.

10
PREPOSITIONS

1

> A PREPOSITION is the first word of a PHRASE
> (See Sections 1 and 19). A preposition is a word
> that is placed or positioned before the other words
> in a phrase.

Examples

1 I had a letter *from* George yesterday.

preposition: *from*
phrase: *from George*

2 We have been hearing voices *in* the haunted room
again.

preposition: *in*
phrase: *in the haunted room*

3 The lock turned *with* a loud click.

preposition: *with*
phrase: *with a loud click*

4 There is a registered letter *for* you.

preposition: *for*
phrase: *for you*

5 Several people were standing *between* him and me.

preposition: *between*
phrase: *between him and me*

6 Invitations were sent *to* Peter and her.

preposition: *to*
phrase: *to Peter and her*

2   A phrase that begins with a preposition is called a **PREPOSITIONAL PHRASE**. (There are other kinds of phrases that do not begin with prepositions. See Section 19.)

3   A preposition introduces a prepositional phrase and it also **LINKS** the phrase to a word used elsewhere in the sentence. It shows that the phrase **REFERS TO** that word.

Examples

1 The QUEUE *outside the station* was moving slowly.

The preposition *outside* links the phrase *outside the station* to the word *queue*. The phrase *outside the station* refers to the word *queue*.

2 He HEARD her voice *with delight*.

The preposition *with* links the phrase *with delight* to the word *heard*. The phrase *with delight* refers to the word *heard*.

4   A prepositional phrase adds to the meaning of the word which it refers to.

Examples

1 The clock was stolen.
The clock *in the hall* was stolen.

The phrase *in the hall* refers to and adds to the meaning of the word *clock* (a noun). The phrase tells us which clock was stolen.

28

2 She wore a ring.
She wore a ring *on her little finger*.

The phrase *on her little finger* refers to and adds to the meaning of the word *wore* (a verb). The phrase tells us where she wore the ring.

3 Jones changed his job.
Jones changed his job *after a year*.

The phrase *after a year* refers to and adds to the meaning of the word *changed* (a verb). The phrase tells us when Jones changed his job.

5 **A preposition and its phrase may be placed immediately next to the word which they refer to.**

Examples

1 The MAN *at the window* shouted something.
2 We live in a HOUSE *with a big garden*.

6 **A preposition and its phrase may be separated from the word which they refer to.**

Examples

1 They TOOK the children *to the seaside*.
2 *During the holidays* we VISITED some friends.

REMEMBER A preposition, like all the other parts of speech, can be recognised only by the WORK that it does IN A SENTENCE. The same word can be a preposition in one sentence and a different part of speech in another.

Examples

1 We walked through the room quietly.

**In that sentence *through* is a preposition.
It introduces the phrase *through the room*.
It links the phrase to the word *walked* (a verb).**

29

2 We walked through quietly.

In that sentence *through* is an adverb.
It does not introduce a phrase.
It modifies the verb *walked*.

Practice 11

Find the prepositions in these sentences. Write out the prepositional phrases. Say which word in the sentence each phrase refers to.

Example

After a long day in the open air the tired travellers returned to their hotel.

preposition	prepositional phrase	word that phrase refers to
after	after a long day	returned
in	in the open air	day
to	to their hotel	returned

1 Fingerprints on the revolver provided the vital clue.
2 We drew very little water from the well last year.
3 People are complaining about her behaviour.
4 Inside the generating plant the temperature rose to a dangerous level.
5 His fury was revealed by his flushed face.
6 We discovered entrants of good quality in the competition.

11
INTERJECTIONS

1 | An INTERJECTION is a word (or words) used in or added to a sentence to express feeling such as surprise, sorrow, dismay, pleasure, and so on.

Examples

1 *Hello!* What's this?
2 *Oh dear*, it's raining again.

2   An interjection plays no part in the grammatical structure of a sentence.

12
THE PARTS OF THE SENTENCE

1
> Every sentence MUST contain a SUBJECT and a PREDICATE (see Section 2).

2
The subject MUST contain a word NAMING the subject (the person, place, thing or idea) about which the predicate says something. That word is called the SUBJECT WORD. The subject word is always a noun or a pronoun (see Sections 4 and 5).

3
The subject MAY also contain
the definite or indefinite article (see Section 6)
and
an adjective (or adjectives) qualifying (describing) the subject word (see Section 6).

the subject	
subject word	definite or indefinite article adjective(s) qualifying subject word

4
The predicate MUST contain a VERB to state what the subject word does or is (see Section 7).

5
The predicate MAY also contain
an adverb (or adverbs) modifying (describing) the verb (see Section 8).

6
The predicate MAY also contain a direct object. (See Section 16.)

7   The predicate MAY also contain an indirect object.
     (See Section 17.)

8   The predicate MAY also contain a complement. (See
     Section 18.)

the predicate				
verb	adverb(s) modifying verb	direct object	indirect object	complement

Those are the parts of the sentence. They are described
in Sections 13–18.

13
SUBJECT WORD AND ADJECTIVES

1

> Since the SUBJECT WORD names (or identifies) the person, place, thing or idea about which the predicate says something, the subject word MUST be
> a noun (a 'naming' word) (see Section 4)
> or
> a pronoun ('standing in' for a noun) (see Section 5).

Examples

A vertical line divides the subject from the predicate. The subject word is in CAPITALS. The verb is in *italics*.

NOUN as subject word.
PASSENGERS | *arrived* at Terminal 3.

PRONOUN as subject word.
THEY | *were sent* through the checkpoints.

2 The subject word may be qualified (described) by an adjective or adjectives.

Example

Tired and angry PASSENGERS | *arrived* at Terminal 3.

3   The subject word may be accompanied by *the* (the
     definite article) or by *a* or *an* (the indefinite article).
     The articles do the same work as an adjective. They
     qualify (describe) a noun. (See Section 6.)

Example

The delayed and dejected PASSENGERS | *arrived* at
Terminal 3.

4   The subject may contain more than one subject word.

Examples

1 GRACE and JEAN | *impressed* the judges.
2 CARS, BUSES and heavy LORRIES | *blocked* the
  narrow street.
3 His SHYNESS and INEXPERIENCE | *handicapped*
  him at the interview.

14
SUBJECT WORD AND VERB

1
> Although the SUBJECT WORD is in the subject of the sentence and the VERB is in the predicate, they are more closely connected with each other than with any other words in the sentence.

2 However many other words there may be in a sentence, the link between the SUBJECT WORD and the VERB provides the sentence with its 'backbone'.

Examples

1 BIRDS | *sing*.
2 Many BIRDS | *sing* beautifully.
3 Many small BIRDS | *sing* beautifully and loudly.
4 Many small BIRDS with dull plumage | *sing* beautifully and loudly at dawn.
5 Many small BIRDS with dull plumage but bright eyes | *sing* beautifully and loudly at dawn in the woodland around the village.

REMEMBER
- The VERB 'belongs to' the SUBJECT WORD.
- The work of the VERB is to state what the SUBJECT WORD does or is.

15
VERB AND ADVERBS

1 | The verb may be modified (described) by an adverb or adverbs (see Section 8).

Example

The fierce spring tide was running strongly.

subject		predicate	
subject word	adjectives qualifying subject word	verb	adverb modifying verb
tide	the fierce spring	was running	strongly

NOTE: The definite article (*the*) is included with the adjectives qualifying the subject word.

2 The adverb or adverbs modifying the verb may be placed next to the verb, or they may be separated from the verb by other words.

Example

Gradually, the terrible losses were openly reported.

Verb: *were reported*
Adverbs modifying verb: *gradually openly*

Practice 12

Split these sentences into their various parts, using the table set out in the example below.

1 Thin people usually eat sparingly.
2 My car's battery failed yesterday.
3 An important letter was not delivered punctually.
4 Down went the gold shares.
5 Five crying children yelled horribly.

Example

The afternoon racing programme will start earlier tomorrow.

subject		predicate	
subject word	adjective(s) qualifying subject word	verb	adverb(s) modifying verb
programme	the afternoon racing	will start	earlier tomorrow

16
DIRECT OBJECT

1

> A VERB that expresses 'doing' (an 'action' verb)
> MAY have a DIRECT OBJECT.

Examples

The VERB is in *italics*.
The DIRECT OBJECT is in CAPITALS.

1 We *drank* LEMONADE.
2 I *am learning* CHINESE.
3 William the Conqueror *defeated* HAROLD.
4 The mountain rescue team *reached* US.
5 He *will post* THEM tomorrow.

2   You can find the direct object by asking the question
    What? or *Whom?* AFTER the verb. The word that
    answers that question is the direct object of the verb.

Examples

1 They play chess.

   They play *What?*   Answer: *chess*.
   chess is the DIRECT OBJECT of the verb *play*.

2 The prime minister likes power.

   The prime minister likes *What?*   Answer: *power*.
   power is the DIRECT OBJECT of the verb *likes*.

3 Her mother spoils Betty.

Her mother spoils *Whom?*   Answer: *Betty*.
***Betty* is the DIRECT OBJECT of the verb *spoils*.**

3   The same verb can be used with or without a direct
     object.

Examples

1 We sang cheerfully.

We sang *What?*   No answer: no direct object.
**The word *cheerfully* is an adverb. It modifies
(describes) the verb *sang*.**

2 We sang some songs cheerfully.

We sang *What?*   Answer: *some songs*.
***some songs* is the DIRECT OBJECT of the verb *sang*.**

3 Arkle ran yesterday.

Arkle ran *What?*   No answer: no direct object.
**The word *yesterday* is an adverb. It modifies
(describes) the verb *ran*.**

4 Arkle ran a superb race yesterday.

Arkle ran *What?*   Answer: *a superb race*.
***a superb race* is the DIRECT OBJECT of the verb *ran*.**

4   The direct object MUST contain a 'naming' word – a
     noun or a pronoun. This is called the DIRECT OBJECT
     WORD.

Example

They caught fish.

The noun *fish* is the direct object word.

5   The direct object word MAY be qualified (described) by an adjective or adjectives.

Example

They caught some big fish.

direct object: *some big fish*
direct object word: *fish*
adjectives qualifying direct object word: *some   big*

Practice 13

Find the direct objects in these sentences. Then divide each direct object into the direct object word and the adjectives qualifying the direct object word. Be careful! One of the sentences does not contain a direct object.

1 This novelist has just written a long and remarkable book.
2 The children explored the deserted house last year.
3 Through the binoculars he saw a weird figure in the distance.
4 At the door we recognised the limping man.
5 The fans were screaming with delight.

17
INDIRECT OBJECT

1

> A VERB that expresses 'doing' (an 'action' verb) MAY have an INDIRECT OBJECT as well as a direct object.

Examples

The VERB is in *italics*.
The indirect object is in CAPITALS.

1 I *gave* MILLY a camera.

| Gave What? | a camera | direct object |
| Gave it To? | MILLY | indirect object |

2 They *offered* HIM a pension.

| Offered What? | a pension | direct object |
| Offered it To? | HIM | indirect object |

3 She *sent* HER BOSS a report.

| Sent What? | a report | direct object |
| Sent it To? | HER BOSS | indirect object |

4 My mother *prepared* US a lovely meal.

| Prepared What? | a lovely meal | direct object |
| Prepared it For? | US | indirect object |

5 The tourists *asked* THE GUIDE the way.

| Asked What? | the way | direct object |
| Asked it From? | THE GUIDE | indirect object |

2 The indirect object MUST contain a 'naming' word – a noun or a pronoun. This 'naming' word is called the INDIRECT OBJECT WORD.

3 The indirect object word MAY be qualified (described) by an adjective or adjectives.

Examples

1 The grateful millionaire left her old college a handsome bequest.

indirect object: *her old college*
indirect object word: *college*
adjectives qualifying indirect object word: *her old*

2 Good-natured neighbours gave the bedridden old man generous help.

indirect object: *the bedridden old man*
indirect object word: *man*
adjectives qualifying indirect object word: *the bedridden old*

Practice 14

Find the direct objects and the indirect objects in these sentences. Identify the direct object word and the indirect object word in each. There are ten direct objects and three indirect objects.

1 Mrs Smith never forgot her retirement day.
2 The directors gave her a gold watch.
3 Her colleagues bought their old friend a fine camera.
4 The whole firm offered its good wishes.
5 They did not forget Mrs Smith's husband.
6 He was given some beautiful flowers and an armchair.
7 People expressed their kind thoughts and good wishes.
8 They gave them both a wonderful day.

18
COMPLEMENT

1

> A verb that expresses 'doing' (an 'action' verb)
> CAN make a complete predicate on its own.
> but
> A verb that expresses 'being' CANNOT make a
> complete predicate on its own.

Examples

'doing' verbs

    1 FISH | *swim*.
    2 Old MEN | *forget*.
    3 The incompetent MINISTER | *resigned*.

'being' verbs

    1 HENRY | *is* ...
    2 MRS JONES | *became* ...
    3 That WORKMAN | *seems* ...
    4 The DOCUMENTS | *were* ...
    5 The moorland ROADS | *are* ...

2 A word or words must be added to COMPLETE the
predicate that a 'being' verb starts to make.

Examples

    1 Henry | is OUR CAPTAIN.
    2 Mrs Jones | became CHAIRPERSON.
    3 That workman | seems VERY CAPABLE.
    4 The documents | were GENUINE.
    5 The moorland roads | are BLOCKED.

3   The word or words that COMPLETE the predicate of a 'being' verb are called the COMPLEMENT of the verb.

4   The complement may be a noun or a pronoun or an adjective.

Examples

The VERB is in *italics*.
The COMPLEMENT is in CAPITALS.

noun as complement
1 Richard II *became* KING in 1377.

pronoun as complement
2 That *is* MINE.

adjective as complement
3 You *are being* OBSTINATE.

5   The complement refers back to and describes the subject of the sentence.

Examples

1 That new process was Brown's idea.

The complement *Brown's idea* refers back to and describes the subject (*That new process*).

2 The rear seats seem cramped.

The complement (*cramped*) refers back to and describes the subject (*The rear seats*).

REMEMBER

complement	direct object
• used with a 'being' verb	used with a 'doing' (an 'action') verb
• refers back to and describes the subject of the sentence	names (identifies) the person, place, thing, or idea that receives the action of the verb

Practice 15

Find the complements and the direct objects in these sentences. Be careful! One of the sentences contains neither a complement nor a direct object.

1 We have not yet discovered a cure for the common cold.
2 A bewildering number of remedies comes on the market every year.
3 A breakthrough seems as far away as ever.
4 Sufferers from this annoying complaint become depressed.
5 A fortune and universal thanks await the discoverer of a cure.

19
PHRASES

<table>
<tr>
<td>1</td>
<td>A PHRASE is a group of words (two or more) that does not make complete sense ON ITS OWN. A phrase adds to (enlarges) the meaning of a sentence. (See Section 1.)</td>
</tr>
</table>

Examples

1 The flowers *in that red pot* need water.
2 We parked our car *by the roadside.*
3 There is a bridge *across the river* here.
4 She read the book *with great excitement.*
5 *Last night* I wrote some letters.
6 *Sleeping soundly* they did not hear the alarm.
7 This engine is noisy *driven hard.*
8 *To sing well* requires a good voice and training.

2   A phrase MAY begin with a preposition (see Section 10), but many phrases do NOT. Four of the phrases in the examples just given do not begin with a preposition: *Last night* (5); *Sleeping soundly* (6); *driven hard* (7); *To sing well* (8).

3   In the sentence in which it is used a phrase does the work of
>   an adjective
>   or
>   an adverb
>   or
>   a noun.

A phrase is
> either
> an adjective phrase
> or
> an adverb phrase
> or
> a noun phrase.

Examples

adjective phrases

1 The trees *in the park* are losing their leaves.

The phrase *in the park* qualifies (describes) the noun *trees*.

2 *Running fast* they caught the last bus.

The phrase *Running fast* qualifies (describes) the pronoun *they*.

3 We heard John *making a terrible din*.

The phrase *making a terrible din* qualifies (describes) the noun *John*.

4 *Hoping to get good seats* we arrived early.

The phrase *Hoping to get good seats* qualifies (describes) the pronoun *we*.

5 *Worried by the rumours* the investors withdrew their money.

The phrase *Worried by the rumours* qualifies (describes) the noun *investors*.

adverb phrases

1 *This week* we are expecting visitors.

The phrase *This week* modifies (describes) the verb *are expecting*.

2 She has gone *to buy a computer.*

The phrase *to buy a computer* modifies (describes) the verb *has gone*. (It states why – for what purpose – she has gone.)

3 The programme resumed *after a short delay.*

The phrase *after a short delay* modifies (describes) the verb *resumed*.

4 The selectors made a good choice *in the circumstances.*

The phrase *in the circumstances* modifies (describes) the verb *made*.

5 I closed the window *because of the noise in the street.*

The phrase *because of the noise in the street* modifies (describes) the verb *closed*.

6 *Considering his age* he did surprisingly well.

The phrase *Considering his age* modifies (describes) the verb *did*.

noun phrases

1 *To eat greedily* is unpleasant and harmful.

The phrase *To eat greedily* is the subject of the verb *is*.

2 We were told *to save electricity.*

The phrase *to save electricity* is the direct object of the verb *were told*.

3 My aim is *to travel comfortably.*

The phrase *to travel comfortably* is the complement of the verb *is*.

49

4 *Smoking in bed* is a fire risk.

The phrase *Smoking in bed* is the subject of the verb *is*.

5 We enjoyed *swimming in the hot weather*.

The phrase *swimming in the hot weather* is the direct object of the verb *enjoyed*.

6 *Using worn tyres* cost the driver a heavy fine.

The phrase *Using worn tyres* is the subject of the verb *cost*.

REMEMBER The same phrase can do one job in one sentence and a different job in another.

Examples

1 Jane had a letter *from London*.

from London is an adjective phrase qualifying (describing) the noun *letter*.

2 Jane will travel *from London*.

from London is an adverb phrase modifying (describing) the verb *will travel*.

3 *Working long shifts* they repaired the bridge.

Working long shifts is an adjective phrase qualifying (describing) the pronoun *they*.

4 *Working long shifts* made them tired and bad tempered.

Working long shifts is a noun phrase; subject of the verb *made*.

Practice 16

Find the phrases in these sentences. Describe the work that each phrase does.

1 You can put your clothes in this drawer.
2 The furniture in this room will be sold tomorrow.
3 Planning to get away early they set their alarm clock.
4 Not having an answer from the hotel worried us.
5 That shop is selling excellent shoes marked down at bargain prices.
6 Fred seems to be getting better.
7 Plotted in secret for more than six months the prisoners' escape was a complete surprise to the authorities.
8 To her friends, Liz seemed calm.
9 The dress was finished in time for the wedding.

20
NUMBER

1

> Nouns and pronouns are either SINGULAR in number or PLURAL in number.

2   When a noun or pronoun is SINGULAR it names ONE person, place, thing or idea.
    When a noun or pronoun is PLURAL it names MORE THAN ONE person, place, thing or idea.

Examples

Singular

| fisherman | book | I | she | interest |

Plural

| fishermen | books | we | they | interests |

3   When the subject word is singular the verb must be singular. When the subject word is plural the verb must be plural.
    As the grammar rule states: 'The verb AGREES WITH its subject word in number.'

Examples

1 Two pints ARE delivered every morning.
2 A crate of bottles IS delivered every morning.
3 I AM going by train.
4 We ARE going by car.

21
PERSON

1

> There are three 'persons':
>   first
>   second
>   third.

Example

I (first person) want to talk to YOU (second person) about HER (third person).

2   Each of the three persons may be either singular or plural.

Example

WE (first person plural) have invited HIM (third person singular) but not THEM (third person plural).

3   The verb must be of the same NUMBER as its subject word. (See Section 20.)
    The verb must also be in the same PERSON as its subject word.
    As the grammar rule states: 'The verb AGREES WITH its subject word in number and in person.'

Examples

1 I (first person singular) *am* going away tomorrow.
2 She (third person singular) *is* going away tomorrow.
3 They (third person plural) *are* going away tomorrow.
4 We (first person plural) *run* this engine on gas.
5 This engine (third person singular) *runs* on gas.

22
CASE

1

> Each pronoun in a sentence is in one of three CASES.
> It is
>> either in the NOMINATIVE case
>> or in the ACCUSATIVE case
>> or in the GENITIVE case.

Examples

1 He (NOMINATIVE case) brought a message for Peter and me (ACCUSATIVE case).
2 I (NOMINATIVE case) like Mary's idea better than yours (GENITIVE case).

2 A pronoun is either nominative or accusative or genitive according to the WORK that it does IN A SENTENCE.

3 The SUBJECT WORD is in the NOMINATIVE CASE.

Examples

1 *I* rang Peter.
2 *We* were pleased.

4 The DIRECT OBJECT WORD is in the ACCUSATIVE CASE.

Examples

1 They chose *him*.
2 Peter rang *me*.

54

5   The INDIRECT OBJECT WORD is in the ACCUSATIVE
    CASE.

Examples

1   They gave *me* presents.
2   Their uncle sent *them* a cheque.

6   A PRONOUN in a PREPOSITIONAL PHRASE is in the
    ACCUSATIVE CASE.

Examples

1   This house is too big for *us*.
2   She divided the sweets carefully between *her* and
    me.

7   A POSSESSIVE pronoun is in the GENITIVE CASE.

Examples

1   The Brown's house is smaller than *ours*.
2   That is the girls' room, this is *mine*.

8   NOUNS do NOT have special forms to show whether
    they are NOMINATIVE or ACCUSATIVE.

Examples

1   The sharp-eyed *thief* recognised the disguised
    detective.

    subject word: *thief*   **nominative case**
    direct object word: *detective*   **accusative case**

2   The sharp-eyed *detective* recognised the disguised
    thief.

    subject word: *detective*   **nominative case**
    direct object word: *thief*   **accusative case**

9   NOUNS DO have special forms to show that they are in the GENITIVE CASE.

Examples

1 That is my younger *girl's* school.

   girl's: singular noun in genitive case

2 The *girls'* new shoes were expensive.

   girls': plural noun in genitive case

3 The women beat the *men's* team.

   men's: plural noun in genitive case

NOTE: A noun in the genitive case does the work of an adjective.

Examples

1 ... younger girl's school

   girl's qualifies (describes) noun *school*

2 ... girls' new shoes

   girls' qualifies (describes) noun *shoes*

3 ... men's team

   men's qualifies (describes) noun *team*

10   Personal pronouns have special forms to show whether they are in the NOMINATIVE CASE or in the ACCUSATIVE CASE or in the GENITIVE CASE.

the personal pronouns			
person and number	nominative	accusative	genitive
1st person singular	I	me	mine
2nd person singular	you	you	yours
3rd person singular	he/she/it	him/her/it	his/hers/its
1st person plural	we	us	ours
2nd person plural	you	you	yours
3rd person plural	they	them	theirs

Examples

1 *He* recognised *him*.

   He: personal pronoun as subject word: nominative case
   him: personal pronoun as direct object word: accusative case

2 Invitations were sent to Henry and *us*.

   us: personal pronoun in prepositional phrase: accusative case

3 Put your coat with *mine*.

   mine: personal pronoun showing possession: genitive case

23
GENDER

1

> English grammar has no complicated rules about the GENDER of nouns – whether they are 'masculine', 'feminine' or 'neuter'.

2   Gender in English grammar is simply a matter of common sense.

Examples

1 *My mother* had a lot of cards on *her* birthday.
2 *My father* often works in *his* greenhouse. *It* gives *him* a lot of interest.

24
ANSWERS TO PRACTICE EXERCISES

Practice 1

1 3 5 6 8 11

Practice 2

John Brown left his keys in his car. Then he slammed the driver's door with the catch down. He was locked out. The local garage could not supply a duplicate key for that particular model. He made enquiries at the police station. After a long time they opened the car door with a lot of trouble.

Practice 3

	subject	predicate
1	diesel engines	are usually reliable
2	the judges	as yet have not announced their decision
3	we	are open until eight tonight
4	his cooking	has improved
5	the two parts of every sentence	are the subject and the predicate

Practice 4

1 Jack   fever   cough   doctor   illness
2 Archimedes   problems   wisdom

Practice 5

1 His	qualifies *record*
ten	qualifies *years*
2 fresh	qualifies *flowers*
that	qualifies *room*
hot	qualifies *room*
3 many	qualifies *people*
your	qualifies *party*
birthday	qualifies *party*
4 What	qualifies *car*
5 Their	qualifies *house*
lovely	qualifies *house*

Practice 6

1 pronoun:	yours
adjective:	that
2 pronouns:	I his hers
adjectives:	Their excellent
3 pronouns:	I this
adjective:	that
4 pronouns:	he little
adjectives:	much very (note that the adjective *very* qualifies the pronoun *little*)
5 pronoun:	Anybody
adjectives:	this rotten

Practice 7

Jo   London   maps   streets   squares   parks   capital familiarity   confidence

Practice 8

1	have been built	subject *ships*
2	looks	subject *she*
3	has been eaten	subject *all the food*
4	will be closed	subject *the store*
5	will need	subject *you*

Practice 9

1	badly yesterday	verb *was coughing*
2	now	verb *know*
3	once	verb *ring*
4	stationary overhead	verb *remained*
5	finally	verb *abandoned*
6	where	verb *is*

Practice 10

1 and but   2 or   3 Neither nor

Practice 11

	preposition	prepositional phrase	word that phrase refers to
1	on	on the revolver	fingerprints
2	from	from the well	drew
3	about	about her behaviour	are complaining
4	inside	inside the generating plant	rose
	to	to a dangerous level	rose
5	by	by his flushed face	was revealed
6	of	of good quality	entrants
	in	in the competition	discovered

61

Practice 12

subject		predicate	
subject word	**adjective(s) qualifying subject word**	**verb**	**adverb(s) modifying verb**
1 people	thin	eat	usually sparingly
2 battery	my car's	failed	yesterday
3 letter	an important	was delivered	not punctually
4 shares	the gold	went	down
5 children	five crying	yelled	horribly

Practice 13

	direct object	*direct object word*	*adjectives qualifying direct object word*
1	a long and remarkable book	book	a long remarkable
2	the deserted house	house	the deserted
3	a weird figure	figure	a weird
4	the limping man	man	the limping

Practice 14

	direct object	*indirect object*
1	her retirement DAY	
2	a gold WATCH	HER
3	a fine CAMERA	their old FRIEND
4	its good WISHES	
5	Mrs Smith's HUSBAND	
6	some beautiful FLOWERS an ARMCHAIR	
7	their kind THOUGHTS good WISHES	
8	a wonderful DAY	THEM both

Practice 15

1 direct object   *a cure for the common cold*
2 neither
3 complement   *as far away as ever*
4 complement   *depressed*
5 direct object   *the discoverer of a cure*

Practice 16

	phrase	kind and function
1	in this drawer	adverb phrase modifying verb *can put*
2	in this room	adjective phrase qualifying noun *furniture*
3	Planning to get away early	adjective phrase qualifying pronoun *they*
4	Not having an answer from the hotel	noun phrase subject of verb *worried*
5	marked down at bargain prices	adjective phrase qualifying noun *shoes*
6	to be getting better	adjective phrase qualifying noun *Fred* and functioning as complement of verb *seems*
7	Plotted in secret for more than six months	adjective phrase qualifying noun *escape*
	to the authorities	adverb phrase modifying verb *was*
8	To her friends	adverb phrase modifying verb *seemed*
9	in time for the wedding	adverb phrase modifying verb *was finished*